LET ME TELL YOU ABOUT MOSES

LET ME TELL YOU ABOUT MOSES

AN EXPERIENCE OF ISRAEL

Texts by Eric Blau

Photographs by Marjorie Jackson Baum

THE BOBBS-MERRILL COMPANY, INC.
INDIANAPOLIS · NEW YORK

FOR JULIA, MY MOTHER,
AND
LILLIAN, MY SISTER

The Bobbs-Merrill Company, Inc.
Indianapolis • New York

CONTENTS

LET ME TELL YOU ABOUT MOSES

FOR NORMA AND SIMON

Love—Let me tell you about Moses
About Moses and Me and the way it was
Love—He was a Jew so long ago
When they put him in the stream to flow
Down the river, down, down, the river
Over the stones and mud and was it God
Or just Pharaoh's daughter her hands in the water
But someone else was floating and it was me
Caught in the bulrushes and lost and lost
In some future time.

Love—Let me tell you about Moses
About Moses and Me and the way it was
Love—He was a Jew when God was new
When he stood with the women by the well
In Midian, down, down, in Midian
Over the land where the hills skipped like lambs
And the water was cool down deep in the pool
But someone else was watching and it was me
Standing at the roadside and lost and lost
In some future time.

Love—Let me tell you about Moses
About Moses and Me and the way it was
Love—He was a Jew when Pharaoh played God
When the ten plagues came down in Egypt land
In Egypt land down, down in Egypt land
Where their lives trickled down into the sand
And with straw and mud they mixed their blood
But someone else was bleeding and it was me
Standing at the roadside and lost and lost
In some future time.

But the Red Sea opened
And the Desert frowned
And Sinai reared up
And Moses climbed
And God came down
The mountain side
The bush it burned
The words were traced
Moses saw God's shoulder
But not God's face
And Moses came down
The mountain side
Moses came down
The mountain side.

Love—Let me tell you about Moses
About Moses and Me and the way it was
Love—He was a Jew as we all must be
When we set out in the stream to flow
Down the river down, down the river
Over stones and mud looking for God
Finding Pharaoh's daughter—soft hands in the water
And she knows that we are floating—it's only us
Caught in the bulrushes and lost and lost
In some future time.

Down the river
Down, down
Down the river
Down, down
In the bulrushes
Lost, lost
In some future time.

JERUSALEM

It is a market place
Brass and lamb skins
And Gates.
It is a market place
Dates and beef sides
And cries.
It is a market place
Open for business
Trading in Coca-Cola
And God.

It is a hustlers' place
Life spilling from sacks
And gourds.
It is a hustlers' place
Crying the glory
Of Thirty Cents.
It is a hustlers' place
Selling memories
Lost beneath the flesh
And the City,
Fouling its nest
Growing over itself
Replacing its walls
Like teeth
Becoming false
Placing all Gods
Before me
Splitting one saviour
In two equal parts
Of Bone and Tears
Below the wooden ramp
Of the indoor Calvary
The metrodome of the ungraspable death...

Barring another saviour
From the Golden Gate
With Turkish iron
And a lawn of graves
Brooding from Mount Olive
Looking across the orchards
Of the lucky, waiting well-positioned dead...

And a third saviour glowing
Beneath the Golden Dome
His steed of fire
Eating coals and pawing
His future flight
Across the skies
Of total redemption...

But the peddlers know it all
And you can get six-to-five pick 'em
On any God you call
And only their stalls are filled
With the Flesh, the Blood and the Holy Spirit
And everybody is waiting for Godot
Except the Arabs and the Jews and the Christians
Floating like miracles with gold teeth
In the squares of darkness
They call their own.

It is a market place
Rendered to Caesar and God
Those historic cruising cops
Who make their smiling rounds
Their shoulders brushing
All the narrow stations.

Elijah unrisen in the olive groves
Mohammed lost in the flames
And some bravos dragging Jesus
Out of Town
Because life must go on
And there are things to sell.

I THINK I TOLD YOU ONCE

FOR ELLY STONE, MY WIFE,
HEARING HER SING IN TEL AVIV
FOR THE SOLDIERS OF ISRAEL

I think I told you once
I heard a bird sing
In a Scottish wood.
Just one bird
Caught in the mist
which moved like ribbons
Thru the dwarf trees.
It was alone. It was calling.
(That's what a song is. You know that.
Someone alone. Someone calling.)
The song came
In little bursts
Like a kid's whistle;
The wood bead spinning.
Then, as if all the winds converged,
The sound held,
Extended,
Spinning like glass and silver
Moving among those blind stubby arms.
And I died because the song died.
I was a soldier then
In the comic rig
Of an indexible war.
I sought for my childhood
For the whistle hooked
To the sailor suit
Hung in the window of the past.
But I was looking the wrong way.
It was the self-conscious,
Unself-conscious eye of the soldier poet.
(A leaf!…the secret of life
A tower!…The solitary finger in the dike of heaven
A chestnut!…All the churches and urchins of Paris.
Wondering if Masson would understand
If gentle Eluard would smile…)
But I was looking the wrong way.
It was your sound. It was you,
Alone and calling on the morning
Of a day which would not come
For a very long time.
When I first heard you sing……
But you know now that the wood,
The mist and the bird came back;
I think I told you once.

THE NATION, THE STATE, THE BORDERS, THE OLD OPERA

Perhaps we have come too late across the ocean sea
To the Nation State. It is all overgrown
With the lichen and fungi of dreams
Yet no regrets, no sighs, no sorrows
For in the twenty scattered centuries
Where we have wandered the lights were lit
Not by lights of homes we never knew
But by the bone and blood of bondage
And by those throbbing lamps we have returned...

But it is so small!
As small as all the places of childhood
Crammed stone by stone into the Testament
Here Abraham dropped his knife
Here Joshua stopped the night
Here David. There Solomon.
Isaac, Aaron, Ruth, Moses
The memories of manna
The mountains worn down
And the rubble of the casual
Empty years and for all our yearning
That awful bad joke:
Where have you been lately?
And we are too weary to name
The ghettos which girdle the globe
We are home
And we must go greening the sands
Putting up towers and teaching
The old land the new ways of milk and honey
We fill the air with flowers
Fix all of the unhinged doors
Brush the cobwebs from the caves
And if it is not the storied glory of the Temple
It is at least the sweetness of the shtetl
In a summer without pogroms
And it is all so exquisitely possible
That we quarrel....
We are still a stiffnecked people
Indestructible in tragedy
Magnificent in war
But, Oh, Delilah, Delilah
The softness of Delilah
In the sweet beds of peace
Orgasms preceding thunder
Prologues of blindness and wrath
Until the chained columns are struck
Until we bleed, until we are crushed
Until we are only our remarkable selves
Stuck in the Talmud, Rashi and Gomorrah
Stuck in the implied songs of the chazanim
Stuck like the jawbones of asses
In the crumbling fields of Ashkelon
A dusty stage on the main drag to anybody's destiny

So we face the sea and listen to the wind
Shuffle down the grassy aisles
And think we hear the flautist at his reed
And perhaps the tympanist laying his sticks to the leaves
We applaud, one-handed and echoing
(A little bit of Zen, a little bit of gevalt).
It is an opera—It is an opera
Of prurient vintage but it must be played
Because we have the sets for it
And one tattered copy of the score
And all the parts and some of the musicians
And more players than we can use
And costumes which will not divide
Quite like loaves and fishes
There to the West lies Jordan!
There, where the hills rise, Syrie!
There is the sea and there Egypt!
And the hills are alive with the sound of Philistines
And the arias are second-rate even if they are old
And at the top of our voice we sing
And at the end, behind the massed and bannered stage,
The sun rises.
We have been here before
We have paid the price before
Always at the scalper's rate
Never a twofer, never a freebee
Never, never a subscription seat
Except this time we pay at the box
And there's room inside
It is our very own opera
At long last ours
Not someone else's road show.
(By the way, do you like opera?)
Our State, Our Nation singing
Even as all the States and Nations sing
And the borders, what about the borders,
The blood red lines of agony?
In appropriate pain
They will be set down.
Here, there, somewhere,
And, of course, they will not be right.
Yet once we did bring water out of a stone—
Which falls somewhere between magic and miracle.
That was very long ago.
This is not exactly an encore.
But we are on stage.

FOUR FANTASIES FOR A VERY OLD SHOEMAKER

1·THIS IS THE CENTER OF THE WORLD

This is the center of the world
This has always been so
The sun always rises
In the olive groves
And sets in the sea by the road

This is the center of the world
This has always been so
The Lord always rests here
On the Sabbath night
And listens to men sing His song

This is the center of the world
This has always been so
The wind always washes
The seas of the sky
It plants dreams of peace as it blows

That's all my wisdom, my son, my son
That's all I have to say
A man who is born
At the center of the world
Can never go away

That's all my treasure, my son, my son
All this I leave to you
The night and the morn
At the center of the world
My dream already come true

That's all my belief, my son, my son
All this I bequeath to you
A mighty nation at peace at last
This endless future, this endless past
To do what you're born to do

For this is the center of the world
This has always been so
The sun always rises
In the olive groves
And sets in the sea by the road

This is the center of the world
This has always been so
The Lord always rests here
On the Sabbath night
And listens to men sing His song

This is the center of the world
This has always been so
The wind always washes
The seas of the sky
It plants dreams of peace as it blows

2·JONAH WILL APPEAR

Jonah will appear
Seaweed in his hair
He will smell of the sea
He will stand right there;
—In the belly of the whale
My boots are gone
I need new boots
Or I can't go on
To Jerusalem....

Old Moses will come
With his tablet and rod
He'll be proud and tall
As if he just faced God
—On Sinai, he'll say,
My sandals were torn
I need new sandals
Or I can't go on
To Jerusalem....

Solomon will arrive
As wise as can be
The crown on his head
Resting uneasily
—I can't think, he'll say,
For my feet ache so
I need stout shoes
Or I cannot go
To Jerusalem....

And Oh Praise His Name
The Messiah will sit here
And Oh Praise His Name
He will sit in my chair
And I will wash his feet
In a silver bowl
I will make him sandals
Of burnished gold
Then we'll all go on
To Jerusalem....

David will appear
His harp in his hand
And David will sing
Of the Promised Land
His voice is rich
But his soles are thin
—Please mend my boots
Or I can't go in
To Jerusalem....

Joshua strides on
The trumpets blare
But there are no more wars
Raging anywhere
—Too many victories
Have burst these seams
I need new boots
To march to other dreams
Of Jerusalem....

And, Oh Praise His Name
The Messiah, He will smile
And Oh Praise His name
He will call me His Child
And I will wash his feet
In a silver bowl
And I will make him sandals
Of burnished gold
And we will all go on
We will all go on
We will all go on
To Jerusalem

3·THE ORGAN OF HAZOREAH

In all the Universe, Oh Lord,
On none of your kibbutzim
Could anywhere be found an organ
But one was made, Adonai Elohim,
And it was played at Hazoreah....

In all the Universe, Oh Lord,
On none of your battleground
Could anywhere be found an organ
But one was made with a heavenly sound
And it was played at Hazoreah

In all the Universe, Oh Lord
On none of your Elysian Fields
Could anywhere be found an organ
But one was made and you can hear it peal
When it is played at Hazoreah

4 · WHERE ARE THE ANGELS?

I see your great rivers flow
I see your round moon aglow
I see your fields of wonder grow
In the path of your great hand
I hear your deeps and oceans roar
I see your wingèd creatures soar
I hear your name in song adored
Dear Lord in every hymn
But where are the seraphs,
Where are the angels,
Where are the cherubim?

I see your great cities rise
I see your temples fill the skies
And, lo, your armies multiply
In the path of your great hand
I see your great orb of gold
I see your Universe unfold
I hear your name in song adored
Dear Lord in every hymn
But where are the seraphs,
Where are the angels,
Where are the cherubim?

FOR A BEDOUIN GIRL OF TWELVE WHO GOT MARRIED THE YEAR BEFORE

When I looked to the South
(After you had taken the candy)
It was to look for a ball
Or a bicycle or some signal of childhood
It was not to turn away from you
I wanted to say: the desert would be
A funny place filled with wheels
Although self-propelled red and yellow balls would do
Rolling over lifts and dips in the sand
Or bowling from tree to tree
On the scraggly oasis
Where the growling camel suddenly pissed
Straight down.
It was not to turn away from you
I wanted to say: I'm not really a tourist.
But I could see myself etched on your eyes
And I confessed it to myself
Just as I confessed that you were not a child
Although there were no breasts
Lifting against the burlap wrap
Which embraced you against the rare rain which fell
I wanted to say: Who is your man?
Who paid your father's price?
Who took you into his bed at night?
And did he gently find the way?
But that would have been prying.
I wanted to say: I hope you don't get
Knocked up until you're twenty
Because everything is leather
And downhill after that.
I wanted to say something obvious:
Like why don't you cut out,
Why don't you run? There must be
A better oasis than this one.
But you were smiling and scratched your ass
And I gave you the rest of the candy.

46

AND THE COLONEL'S WIFE SAID......

Let's not make love tonight, Dov
You are unclean and you should sleep
Outside the room, outside the city
With the other men who have their time
Who are letting blood.

You are just returned from Lebanon
You are unclean and you should sleep
Outside the room, outside the city.
The desert wind will dress the wounds
Which death has made.

Let's not make love tonight, Dov
You smell of death and liberation
If you touch my breasts, open my thighs,
I will look away and turn to salt
Although I love you.

Dov, Dov, if you trust the night
Go quickly into the darkness
And I will say three prayers:
That you will rise up at day
That they shall forgive you
That you shall forgive them.

AN INTERVIEW WITH A SOUTHERN APE CONFINED WITH THE ASIAN FLU TO AN OLD ESSENE CAVE

Of course, I am astounded to find you alive and well and living at the Dead Sea.

I'm sick. I'm going to die.

It's only a bad cold; it will pass.

From your mouth to God's ears. Did you drink the water down there? It's awful.

It's unpotable; but there's a fresh water stream running into it.

I stay clear of that. Lots of brush.

There are no lions, no predators.

Where did they go?

Who?

The lions, the lions!

I don't know, really. They haven't been in these parts for centuries.

That's when they get you. Clever, clever, those lions.

But you? Have you got a name? What are you doing here? Nobody has seen you around in twenty million years.

What the hell are you talking about?

It doesn't matter. What is your name?

You're getting obscure.

Your name—what do they call you?

What kind of shit is that? I'm a Southern Ape. Australopithecus. I look around if someone grunts. If it's a broad, I look around quicker. I had a femur bone here. Did you see it?

No.

It was a helluva femur bone. Zok. Take out a full-grown baboon just like that. Also my antelope jaw. Good one. Sharp as a sonuvabitch. Hate to be here with a bad cold and no weapons. You sure there are no lions down at the stream?

Quite sure.

Things are different than they used to be. No lions?

None. Not one.

Hmmm. So what else is new?

Israel. A new state. A new nation.

Herbivorous or carnivorous?

You don't understand. A state. A nation. The first Jewish State in two thousand years.

Not something you eat? Not something that eats you?

No, no. It's a group of people—Jews who have returned here to live.

A troop of apes?

No. No. People. Jewish people like me.

Well, you're an ape of a sort as far as I can see.

Have it that way if you will. People or apes, we have all gathered here in one place to live.

Aha, you have your own territory.

That's right.

Then somebody must be attacking it.

How did you know that?

After a few million years you get to know things. Once you establish territory it gets all the other apes uptight. They simply have got to attack. You know, the territory is always greener on the other side....

Amazing.

And who are you attacking?

Well, we are having certain difficulties with Egypt, Lebanon, Jordan and the Palestinian guerrillas....

Don't take it too seriously. In the end it always works out. The big problem, the really big problem, is the pecking order. You can win all the wars but that only means you sit around the water hole and throw mud at each other. Somebody always wants to be the Big Ape. Then the Deputy Big Apes always want to beat up on the Nothing Apes and eat all the prime antelope cuts and also get the best looking chicks.

I take it that you are not the Big Ape.

And not a Deputy either. And if you must know the truth, I've got lots of lumps on my head. When it comes to eating, it's always antelope giblets. And I can't look at the crotch of a tree without getting horny....

Why don't you leave here? Come down with me and I'll show you the country.

No thanks. Last time I went down I saw those skinny apes writing funny things on round paper. Nuts....

Did you talk to them?

I tried but after a couple of head swoks I said to hell with it. Then I got this cold.

Come out and sit in the sun. You'll get better. The cold will disappear.

No thanks. All I have left is this cold and if I lose that what will be the meaning of life?

Having a cold cannot be the meaning of life. Is that all you have learned in twenty million years?

No.

Well, what have you learned?

That a cold is psychosomatic and the worst thing is not to have a normal sex life.

Is that all? What about Nations? What about God? What about the Destiny of Man?

What the hell are you talking about?

Bigger issues.

Bigger issues are lions. And any ape who goes around saying, "There are no lions," doesn't know his ass from his femur bone....

WHO IS A JEW?

I say Tom McGrath is a Jew
And he will not dare deny it
I cannot speak for his father
Lost on the north forty in Dakota
I cannot speak for his mother
Who may yet light candles to Mary
I am only sure of McGrath
Because of the quality of his tears

I say Rigó Jancsi is a Jew
And he cannot ever deny it
Because he was a Gypsy fiddler
Who died unknown in New York
Widowing a Hungarian Countess—
What's left is some pastry bearing his name
My father told me this when I was small
So Rigó must be a Jew after all

I say that I am a Jew
And I never knew how to deny it
I know it as well as I know God
Or as well as I do not know God
Or almost as well as the Rabbis know God
You must remember me. I came from Ninth Street,
The Upper Ghetto to the North
Where all that was asked of a Jew
Was to survive. *Henaini!*
Here I am after all these years
Still saying it, still insisting,
Not waiting for the Great I Am
Or for Our Teacher or for Our Tormentor
Just being it, just Zenning it.
I say I am a Jew
Who is fool enough to deny it?

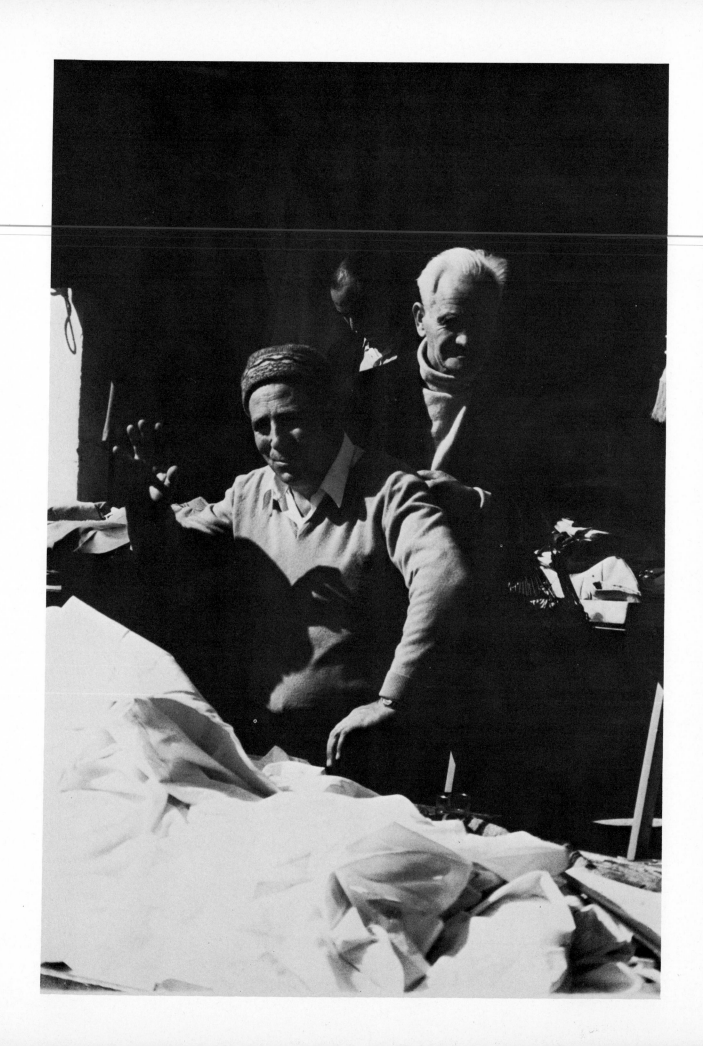

A PRIMER FOR JEWS, NON-JEWS AND OTHERS

1

The Yemenites take four wives
They've done it all their lives
But the Talmud is filled with laws
And each one is a holy cause
Yet the Yemenites are not in sin
Since there's precedent therein
On this score the judges may not be tough
Since four wives, they say, is punishment enough

2

In Jerusalem you cannot kid a Jew
If it isn't very old
Then it's very very new

3

That's how it was with the Crusaders
They caught you now and screwed you later
Thus if you carefully look around
Some Arabs are dark and some are blound

4

The Druzes aren't Arabs
The Druzes aren't Jews
They live in little houses
Which have enormous views

5

At the Hilton in Tel Aviv
People find it hard to live
Not because the food is rotten
Things like that can be forgotten
In the Holy Land one profoundly regrets
That God can be charged American Express

6

There was a little boy from Haifa
Who really couldn't be nicer
When told Israel was antique
Much of it Roman much of it Greek
He accepted the news, his eyes on his shoes
And continued to piss in the creek.

GANDHI'S* PARTY

I went to Gandhi's goddam party
And everyone was there
No one knew when the party started
And nobody seemed to care
We played on flutes and tambourines
We pounded little drums
No one knew why we celebrated
And rumtitumtita tum
I went to Gandhi's goddam party
And it was a hell of a thing
We got high on Carmel brandy
And every Jew can sing
And every Jew can sing

**Ho la dah didah
Ho lah didid dah
dah dah dah**

I went to Gandhi's goddam party
Where we got drunk with dreams
No one knew when the dreams got started
It was long ago it seemed
We played on flutes and tambourines
We pounded little drums
No one knew why we celebrated
And rumtitumtita tum

*Gandhi is the nickname of one of Israel's leading generals.

FOR MY TRIBESMEN ON THE NEW LEFT, THE OLD RIGHT AND THE DEAD CENTER

Or is it only in a dream that we embrace?
In night images occupying sense
From border to border;
Bodies which have no weight, no smells,
Which move in motions too slow or too fast
Over flat maps which designate no roads,
No towns, no tomorrows?
And do we not awake
Each of us alone
In the cold pre-National Halls of Mirrors?
You crying: I love my enemy more than myself...
You crying: I love myself more than my enemy...
You whimpering: Be still, be still,
For my sake, be still....

Reflections. Left-handed statements of light
Bounced once to the eye
To the inner eye
To the dream
Where we embrace in the world we cannot touch

I am, I feel, I am as much as a homing salmon
I am, I feel, I am no less than a turtle
flopping to the sea
I am, I feel, I am no less than lots of
monkeys sucking for the treetop air of home
Yet I do not know where I live

Poor, poor me, out of Abraham, out of Jacob
All American yet well circumcised
With an ear to Paine's drum
With an ear to David's harp
And where in Mao or Marx
Or in *Mein Kampf*
Or in the Talmud
Am I defined?
You will not find me
Among the closet Jews of Cairo
Or Moscow or Washington
Or six-pointed and peaceful
In the synagogues.
I am a Jew
Just a plain Jew
Out of Alexander of Koscord
Out of Julia of Golacs
And going back and back and back
Among the begats without pride
But with so much anger
Because it is still true
That I must show my card to fools
And sew my yellow star upon my sleeve.

70

And what does it all mean?
But that I believe that I am
That I was
That I will be
That I will not be
That I will be again
Or that I will be nothing
If I am not a Jew
And when there was no Israel
I did not need it
And when there was an Israel
I could not surrender it.

ABOUT THE MOUNT OF OLIVES AND THE GREAT ATLANTIC AND PACIFIC TEA COMPANY

Pappa, when I saw the Mount of Olives
I thought of you and I thought of Mamma
And not for a moment was I bitter
Although being bitter comes easily to heart
But the blood pumps and the bile thins out in the stream.

For what are they but graves
Rolling down to the gates and the walls
Jews lying under the green
Box seats on the fifty-yard line
Clean view of the Messiah when he comes...

But Jews lie under every earth
And, God only knows, on how many hills
As you lie on your Mount Moriah
Not that one on which Solomon built
But one of those other Moriahs
Which rise up on old potato fields
Or on bumpy plots the builders left behind
Which somehow fill the bill
For even in these foreign places
Ancient names are magical

On the top of the Mount of Olives, Pappa,
The winter breeze is cool
And the tourists play at eternity
And touch up to God as they look down
And it would be good (for them)
Except for the Arab kids clustered
Around the cars with hands full
Of holiness at about a dime a feel.
They have such sweet faces and sell us
Fortune and good luck and know
That weeping Jews are suckers
And the softest marks to touch....

Over at your place in New Jersey, Pappa,
The ivy in two shades of green
Sends its roots deeply down
To blanket you against the snows
And Mamma waits to take her place
Alongside, beneath the monument.
I don't think she thinks of Mount Olive
It is this place which is nearest heaven
And nearest peace and nearest you.

I suppose that I am satisfied, too,
Although I resent the hard left turn
Off the highway and through the painted gate
To see our name cut into the stone.
The name looks fine, clean and deep,

But I see it and I think
The whole thing is so obscene.

All that way from Koscord,
All those years behind the wheel
Of how many yellow taxicabs
Only to be planted here
Not below the Temple Wall
Not even beneath Omar's Mosque
But beneath the brand of the A&P
Which sits on the hill above
Smiling down in great red thrusts
Shit, Pop, hasn't it always been
That way for us?

Pass the pipe, baby,
This is the destiny bag.
Whose father's ghost goes there among the dunes?

Hey, Ahmad, it is the numbers game
With the sixes and nines gone straight
Hey, Ahmad, it is the numbers game
With the eights jammed up the ass of a corpse
Hey, Ahmad, we are three million killer Jews
Carpeted from sea to sea like locusts
And we will shofar up ten million more
Just in case, in the end, you will wipe us out
(I really think that would be unfortunate
But at least you will have broken the old record.)
Hey, Ahmad, don't shed a tear for us
(Protocols of the Elders of Zion; kikes, you know)
Hey, Ahmad, we know how to die
We're professionals
And quite good at it
Torquemada was a shit kicker.

And here you come!
Two hundred, three hundred million Arabs
Lead by the son of Arafat
And Lorenz of Arabia
(Turn your throat up, old wolf)
Over the hills and through the valleys
Yowling: **ZAP, POW, BAM, SPLAT and PIFF**
We are dead.
Will you bury us?
Where will you bury us?

Ah, Ahmad, what do you think
When you think of that holocaust
Could it go the other way
Could it be us tearing you up?
The equation doesn't reverse.
The Hashemite King will kill more Palestine kids
Than all the Jew Battalions
The Cadillac Sheiks will suck more Arab blood
Into the pipes of thick oblivion
And the newly minted socialists will say the words
Which I have kissed and leave you with the tuna cans
Ah, Ahmad, Power eats people
And Arabs taste as good as Jews...

Ah, Ahmad, what a night is this night
We could walk along the sea road
Picking dates and figs and feeling good
We could be the Middle East
And Juliette could be the sun
And if she were your sister
I would sleep with her
If you understand that this is love.

THE JOURNEY
NOT YET
WINDING DOWN
FOR A.W.S.

1932

In that summer we were young enough
To see the swans on English ponds
And the jungles where Tarzan flew
In special trees; but we secretly knew
That he was Lord Greystoke and impervious
To the dangers stalking post-pubic Jews
In Bridgeport.
In that summer we were young enough
To see the stars in unwrapped skies
And mark them out and claim them all for us,
Our skins tightening for we secretly knew
That the vastness of heaven was cold to the feel
Its hard edge fused to our passing dreams
on Poplar Street.
In that summer we were young enough
To know that we were to be thrown like Dice
Or Odysseus into a diaspora far wider
Than from here to California and that we would go
In white hearses and gray ships to places
Where we were mechanics or fools, doing our thing,
Moving on.

1945
PARIS

So next we meet in Paris
Underneath the Arch
Standing firmly on the tomb
Of the Unknown Soldier;
That was Pappa's war
And your pocket got picked.
And I wept for France
(*Ma patrie, ma belle, mon amour!*)
Oh, the shame, oh, the woe,
That your wallet could be lifted
Beneath the flooding tricolor
And the crosses of Lorraine
(*Tant pis!*)
So we tool around the town of Paris
In a G.I. half-ton truck
And note the Notre Dame
And celebrate our luck.
We never mention the Camps at all
The row on row of bony Jews
The furnace flues did not suck up.
Our nostrils twitch on that air
For forever in the floating dust
Our shit-out-of-luck brothers are there.
The numbers are not tallied yet
And we are already numbed.
So we talk about the Tuileries
And go down to the old Marais
To find the first delicatessen
Which had opened up for trade
And try our rusty Yiddish
In halting household phrase.
You will be gone soon
In your flying machine.
I will go home by boat.
And in the slide of the coming years
We will meet in the graveyards
Where we put our meshpocheh
Down into the earth
And wash our hands and softly talk
Caressing the kinescopes of childhood,
Knowing even as we walk on Main Street,
Bridgeport no longer exists

1971
TEL AVIV

So we meet again in Tel Aviv
You are the same
And you are kind enough
To say I haven't changed
Have I not, now?
And haven't you?
Me? I have kept all these years
To my strange belief in words:
Putting them down, putting them down
Into their own peculiar earth
And waiting too often for an arena
To spring up bravoing,
Saying my name in praise.
But I reap mainly wind and weeds.
Something finally grows but too late
But I am so engaged and go on and hope
To do a few things well
And more and more I long to sit and feel the sun...
But you are surrounded by Israel
By the oranges and the mountains
By the ruins and by the sea
And you have planted marvelous vineyards.
And, yes, yes, of course,
You are still the old mechanic
And you have put together
Thousands of guns
Thousands of planes
Thousands of hard things
But you are the same
A patina of grease, still on your hands.
You are careful still
To rub your nose
With the back of your wrist
Your head is in your secret workshop
So far away from the weeping market place
You are the same.
I have not changed.
We play the game
We have not arranged.
Your hands are filled with birds
You have built a nation
My head is filled with words
Perhaps a song or two.
We part now and exchange gifts
You have given me Israel
And I have given you this....